DISCOVER
Ancient
EGYPT

Discover Ancient Egypt
Published in 2006 by
Hinkler Books Pty Ltd
17–23 Redwood Drive
Dingley, Victoria, 3172, Australia

HINKLER BOOKS

© Hinkler Books Pty Ltd 2006

Author: Heather Hammonds
Design: JM Artworks
Cover Design: Peter Tovey Stud'
Prepress: Graphic Print Group

2 4 6 8 10 9 7 5 3
07 09 11 10 08

ISBN: 1 7415 7524 9

Printed and bound in China.

Contents:

Introduction

*W*elcome to the mysterious and exciting world of ancient Egypt! Thousands of years ago, ancient Egyptians lived in busy cities and towns along the banks of the River Nile, in North Africa. Their huge stone pyramids, the priceless golden treasures they created, the artwork and writing they left behind for us to discover, and their mysterious mummies have fascinated people over the centuries. Many have travelled to Egypt in search of the secrets of the ancient Egyptians.

The people of ancient Egypt were very advanced for their time. While people in many other parts of the world were living in small primitive villages, the ancient Egyptians had created a form of writing called hieroglyphs, were studying astronomy and mathematics, and building those pyramids that are still standing today. They were ruled by powerful kings, called **pharaohs**, who were treated like gods, and the pyramids were built as **tombs** for these kings.

Now you can learn about the ancient Egyptians and how they lived, with this book and activity box. There are pages to read and activities to do, and there's lots of fun to be had!

TIP!
When you see a word in **bold**, you can look up its meaning in the back of this book.

The Land of the Pharaohs

Ancient Egyptians lived on the River Nile, which is the longest river on Earth. Very little rain falls in Egypt and much of the country is desert, so they depended on the Nile for all of their water. Each year the Nile flooded from around June to September, washing down a type of soil called silt, from far-away mountains. This made the soil around the edges of the Nile very fertile and allowed the ancient Egyptians to grow lots of food. Because of this, their civilisation flourished. Ancient Egyptians also used the Nile for transport, travelling along it to different towns and cities by boat. Some boats were made of wood but many were made of reeds.

Ancient Egyptian royalty and other wealthy people lived in palaces and large houses, but most people lived in much smaller homes, made of mud bricks that had been dried by the sun. The homes had flat roofs where people cooked their meals and also slept. Towns were built near the Nile, on high ground. Sometimes hills of sand were used as barriers, to protect the houses from flooding.

FACT!
Today, the River Nile does not flood because large dams have been built along the river.

The ancient Egyptian civilisation lasted for thousands of years. In early times, Egypt was divided into two countries, called Upper and Lower Egypt. Then around 3100 BC a great ruler, the Pharaoh (king) Menes, united the two countries into one Egypt.

He built his palace on the border of the two countries and called it the Palace of the White Wall.

Ancient Egyptians are famous for the pyramids they built as tombs for their rulers. The first pyramid was built in 2650 BC. Over the next thousand years around 100 pyramids were built. After this time, the ancient Egyptians buried most of their rulers in a desert valley, called The Valley of the Kings.

Ancient Egypt was invaded by Greece in 332 BC and then, in 30 BC, it became part of the Roman **Empire**, and was ruled by the Romans. During this time, much of ancient Egyptian culture was forgotten. It was the end of an amazing civilisation.

FACT!

Different times in ancient Egyptian history have different names:

Time when the pyramids were built

Old Kingdom	3100–2125 BC
First Intermediate Period	2125–1975 BC
Middle Kingdom	1975–1640
Second Intermediate Period	1640–1550 BC
Rulers buried in the Valley of the Kings	
New Kingdom	1550–1075 BC
Third Intermediate Period	1075–715 BC
Late Period	715–332 BC

Investigating Ancient Egyptians

*W*ow! Imagine travelling to Egypt and studying ancient Egyptian history. Well, Egyptologists do just that. Egyptologists are **archaeologists** who study everything about ancient Egyptian civilisation. Much has been learnt about ancient Egyptians and their amazing civilisation through the work of Egyptologists.

Egyptologists learn about ancient Egypt in many different ways. They:

• carefully excavate, or dig up, ancient towns and villages
• study ancient Egyptian writing and work out what is written
• study paintings and other artwork showing ancient Egyptian life
• search for, and open, the tombs of ancient kings and queens
• study mummies – the preserved remains of ancient Egyptians.

FACT!

In the 1800s and early 1900s, the first Egyptologists opened ancient Egyptian tombs, took the treasures from them and sold them! They did not care about ancient Egyptian history. Egyptologists today carefully preserve any treasures they find and give them to the Egyptian government.

In past times, Egyptologists had to rely on digging only to help them find hidden tombs, or uncover lost Egyptian cities. They spent many hours in the hot sun at excavation sites, working to find hidden treasures from the past.

Today, Egyptologists still spend lots of time at excavation sites, digging up ancient Egyptian **artefacts**. However, they also have lots of modern equipment to make their job much easier.

They use:

• metal detectors, to help them find metal objects beneath the ground
• ground-penetrating radar, to help them see tombs and tunnels beneath the ground
• aerial photographs taken from planes and satellites to help them find old town sites
• satellites
• robots and small cameras, to help them inspect small underground spaces
• computers to help them create site plans of tombs, cities and other ancient places.

The treasures of ancient Egypt must be preserved, after Egyptologists find them.

The desert sands of Egypt are very dry, so many objects that have been found over the years have been well preserved. Mummies of long-dead kings have been found in very good condition. Wooden items from tombs that are thousands of years old have also been found, looking almost new. So have ancient paintings on tomb walls. Even food such as bread and fruit placed in tombs has been preserved. However, as soon as these treasures are discovered and exposed to the air and sunlight, they start to rot.

Many items from ancient Egypt are stored in museums, to preserve them and keep them in good condition. Then everyone who visits the museum will be able to see them for many more years to come!

FACT!

Just picking up an ancient object that has been hidden inside a tomb for thousands of years can damage it, because of oil and moisture on our skin. Egyptologists usually wear gloves when examining ancient artefacts in museums.

ACTIVITY

Uncovering Hidden Relics

*E*gyptologists dig down through layers of sand and stone to find amazing royal tombs or ancient cities. Now you can uncover your own Egyptian relic with the ancient sand-encrusted artefact we have provided in this activity box!

You will need:

• sand-encrusted artefact from this activity box   • small brush from this activity box
• digging tool from this activity box

1. Place the sandstone block on a large sheet of newspaper, to catch the sand you scrape away.

2. Use the digging tool to gently scrape away the top surface of the sandstone block. Then brush the block clean. Do this gently – remember, Egyptologists must work slowly and carefully so they don't damage any artefacts beneath the stone they are excavating.

3. Continue digging and brushing through more layers of sandstone. As you near the centre of the block, be extra careful!

4. Uncover your ancient Egyptian artefact. Brush the last of the sand from it and see what you have found. Then store your relic in a safe place and handle it carefully, just like a real Egyptologist!

Mysterious Mummies

*M*ummies are the preserved remains of people or animals that have died. In ancient Egypt, people believed in an afterlife - a life after death. They believed that after they died, they would still need their body and things such as clothes and food. Those who could afford to had their bodies preserved by **embalming**, so they could use them again after death. The internal organs were removed from the bodies and placed in special jars. Then the bodies were dried out with natron, a special kind of salt. The bodies were filled with grasses, herbs, sawdust or linen, and wrapped in linen bandages.

Ancient Egyptians who were poor and could not afford to be embalmed were buried in the desert, where their bodies naturally became mummies in the hot, dry conditions.

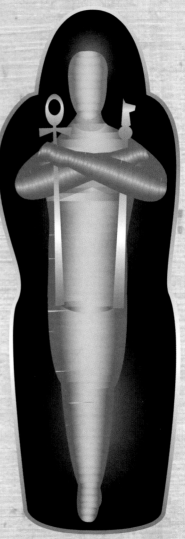

FACT!

Mummies discovered by the first Egyptologists were often unwrapped so that everyone could see the remains of the long-dead Egyptians. This damaged the fragile remains. Today, Egyptologists rarely unwrap mummies. Instead, they use modern medical scanners and x-ray machines to examine the mummies, inside their bandages!

*A*ncient Egyptian kings and queens, and other important ancient Egyptians, were buried in tombs containing lots of amazing treasures so that they could use them in the afterlife. Egyptologists have learnt much of what they know about ancient Egyptian life by studying these treasures, as well as ancient Egyptian writing or hieroglyphs, which were written on the walls inside the tombs of kings and queens.

After a royal ancient Egyptian died, they were embalmed. This took around seventy days. A face was carefully painted onto the bandaged mummy, or it was often given a burial mask. Then it was placed inside three wooden coffins. The first coffin was body-shaped and brightly decorated with pictures and writing that often explained who the dead person was. The second coffin was also body shaped, but more simply decorated. The third coffin was a rectangle shape. The coffins containing the mummy were then placed inside a stone coffin, called a sarcophagus, inside the mummy's tomb. The mummy's tomb was then sealed, along with all the treasures.

FACT!
Hundreds of years before Egyptologists came to explore them, tomb raiders stole lots of the treasures from many ancient Egyptian tombs. They took the precious gold, jewels, statues and other objects that had once belonged to the wealthy Egyptian royalty.

Amazing Pyramids

Ancient Egyptians are most famous for the amazing pyramids they built as tombs for their kings. The pyramids were built with thousands and thousands of huge stone blocks, some of which weighed around fifty tonnes. The stone blocks were pulled along on rollers by gangs of workers. The outer walls of the pyramids were lined with more blocks of limestone, and polished until they shone. They must have been an incredible sight when they were first completed, shining in the hot Egyptian sun! Most pyramids took twenty to thirty years to build and thousands of people worked on them.

Inside the pyramids were passageways and chambers for storing all the goods that it was thought the Egyptian king would need after he had died, in the afterlife. There was also a large burial chamber for the king, along with more possessions.

FACT!

Each pyramid was part of a larger walled-in group of buildings, which included temples and also burial chambers for less important members of the royal family.

The pyramids of Giza are the most famous pyramids in Egypt. The Great Pyramid of Cheops, in Giza, was built by the Pharaoh Cheops. It is the largest stone building in the world! It is 146 metres high and each side is 230 metres at its base. It is also one of the Seven Wonders of the World.

Very little is known about the mysterious Pharaoh Cheops, as the pyramid had been broken into and his tomb robbed of all its treasures before Egyptologists discovered it.

There are several shafts inside the pyramid through which stars can be seen, and it is thought they were built so that the dead king could see some of the star **constellations** in the sky. Smaller pyramids and temples are built nearby, as part of the pyramid complex.

Today, thousands of people travel from all over the world to visit the pyramids of Giza.

ACTIVITY

Make a pyramid paperweight

*Y*ou can make a pyramid paperweight, to remind you of the amazing pyramids of ancient Egypt. This paperweight is made from salt dough and will keep for a very long time.

Salt dough recipe

You will need:
• 4 ¹/₂ cups flour • 2 cups salt

• 4 teaspoons of yellow non-toxic powder paint (if desired) • 1 teaspoon vegetable oil

• 1 ¹/₂ to 2 cups water • large mixing bowl and spoon • oven and baking tray

• an adult's help

1. Mix the flour, salt and powder paint together in the bowl.

2. Add the vegetable oil together with 1 ¹/₂ cups of water and stir well until the mixture becomes a firm dough. Add a little more water, if necessary.

3. Knead the dough until it is smooth. It is now ready to use.

Once you have made the salt dough, you can start building your pyramid!

The pyramid paperweight

You will need:

• 1 quantity of salt dough • ruler
• table knife • flat surface to work on

1. Knead and roll a piece of salt dough about the size of a tennis ball on a flat surface to form a smooth egg shape.

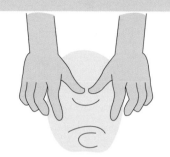

2. Stand the egg shape on its end and push gently down on it, so that the bottom part spreads out to form a cone shape.

3. Use the knife to smooth four sides into the cone. You should now have a pyramid shape.

4. Measure each of the four sides at the base of the pyramid to make sure that they are equal, just like the real ancient Egyptian pyramids.

5. Use the knife to score lines on the sides of your pyramid, so that they look like bricks.

6. When you have made your pyramid, ask an adult to dry it in an oven at 100° C (200° F) for between three and six hours, depending on the size of the paperweight. Larger paperweights or other salt dough models will need more cooking time.

TIP!
Try making other ancient Egyptian artefacts out of salt dough, like mummies or Egyptian statues. They make great gifts!

The Valley of the Kings

uring the time in ancient Egyptian history known as The New Kingdom, from 1550 BC, Egyptian pharaohs were buried in special tombs dug underground, instead of pyramids. These tombs were dug into the sides of a valley known today as the Valley of the Kings, in desert country near the River Nile. Other members of Egyptian royalty were also buried in the Valley of the Kings. Egyptologists have discovered more than sixty five tombs in the valley so far.

Tombs in the Valley of the Kings were not built in the same way as pyramids. They were usually built with three main corridors, an antechamber (entrance chamber) and a sunken burial chamber containing the royal person's sarcophagus and coffins. Other small corridors often led to smaller rooms and chambers.

FACT!
Today, visitors can go to the Valley of the Kings and visit many of the underground tombs.

Tombs in the Valley of the Kings were also filled with goods that royalty might need or want in the afterlife, such as food, clothing, furniture, jewellery and beautiful statues. Walls were decorated with paintings and ancient Egyptian writing.

It is believed that royal tombs were built in the Valley of the Kings because they were able to be hidden, and harder to rob. However, many tombs were broken into and precious goods stolen from them long ago, before modern Egyptologists discovered them.

In the 1700s and 1800s, Egyptologists from England and France began to visit the Valley of the Kings and explore some of the tombs. However, many of the tombs were undiscovered – hidden under the rock and sand in the valley. Egyptologists knew there must be more tombs to be found. They went on expeditions and searched for them, hoping to find a tomb that had not been robbed and still contained all the pharaoh's riches...

The Riches of Tutankhamun

The most famous tomb to be discovered in the Valley of the Kings belonged to the pharaoh Tutankhamun. Tutankhamun became king when he was very young - probably aged eight or nine. He ruled for a short time and then died suddenly when he was still a teenager, at only nineteen years old.

In 1922 Egyptologist Howard Carter discovered Tutankhamun's tomb. It had been hidden under ancient workmen's huts and although tomb raiders had twice broken into it hundreds of years earlier, many of the goods inside it had been left behind.

Carter found many priceless treasures inside Tutankhamun's tomb, including beautiful statues, a golden throne and even ancient flowers! Most importantly, Carter found Tutankhamun's mummy and his solid gold death mask inside his undisturbed coffins.

FACT!
For a long time, Egyptologists thought Tutankhamun was murdered. Now modern scanners have shown he badly broke his leg not long before he died. His leg probably became infected and that is why he died.

After Howard Carter opened Tutankhamun's tomb, rumours of a mummy's curse began to spread. It was said that the mummy was taking revenge on those who had opened its tomb!

First, Carter's pet canary was supposedly swallowed by a snake on the day he opened the tomb. A snake could be seen on the king's golden death mask. Also, Carter was employed by a wealthy Englishman, Lord Carnarvon, to look for Tutankhamun's tomb. A few weeks after the tomb was opened, Lord Carnarvon suddenly died. Other people who helped open the tomb were also supposed to have died.

A newspaper printed a curse that was supposedly found in the tomb. It said: "They who enter this sacred tomb shall be visited by swift wings of death."

Of course, the mummy's curse was not true. There was no curse in the tomb – the newspaper made it up. The canary did not get eaten by a snake and Lord Carnarvon died after a mosquito bit him on the cheek and the bite became infected! Other people closely connected with opening Tutankhamun's tomb did not die suddenly, either. But it was a good story!

ACTIVITY

Make a golden mask

𝒰se the picture of Tutankhamun's death mask as a guide to make your own beautiful mask. This project takes time, but it is well worth it!

You will need:
· a balloon · newspaper and white paper
· scissors and masking tape · craft glue and a bowl
· gold and blue craft paint and a brush
· cardboard roll and a sheet of thin craft cardboard

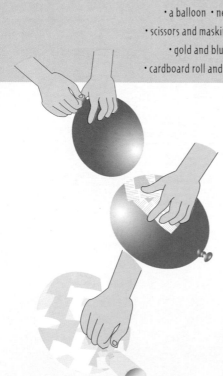

1. First, blow up the balloon.

2. Cut the newspaper and white craft paper into lots of small squares.

3. Now put some glue into the bowl and dip the newspaper squares into the glue.

4. Stick the newspaper squares onto the balloon, until the balloon is covered. Let it dry and then stick another layer of newspaper squares onto the balloon.

5. When the newspaper is dry, use glue or masking tape to stick the cardboard roll onto the chin of the mask. Leave some room at the base of the mask, as you will cut the base back later so that you can fit your head through it.

ACTIVITY

6. Cut a circle from the craft cardboard. Cut the base of the circle off, as shown. Then cut the circle in half and use tape or glue to secure half to each side of the mask.

7. Put some more glue in the bowl, dip the white paper squares into the glue and then stick them to the mask, including the cardboard roll and circle halves.

8. When the mask has dried, use the scissors to pop the balloon inside the mask.

9. Cut around the base of the mask, so it fits over your head. Or you may wish to cut the back off the mask, so it just covers the front of your face. (If you do this, you will need to secure it with some string or elastic when you wear it by poking a hole in each side of the mask.) Then cut some eye holes and a mouth hole too, if you wish.

10. Finally, use the gold and blue paints to decorate your mask!

Hieroglyphs – Read All About It!

*M*uch of what Egyptologists have learned about ancient Egypt has come from the hieroglyphs found on the walls of the tombs of the pharaohs, in temples and on official **documents**. Hieroglyphs are a form of ancient picture writing used by the Egyptians of long ago.

Ancient Egyptians actually had two forms of writing. Hieroglyphs were used for writing on important occasions. Another type of writing, called hieratic writing, was a shortened version of hieroglyphs that was much quicker to write. This was used as everyday writing.

Only some people could write in ancient Egyptian times. These people were called scribes. Scribes trained under other scribes to learn their craft and it took several years to become a scribe. Most scribes were men.

FACT!
Hieroglyphs were often written from the right to left – the reverse direction to the way English is written today.

For many years, early Egyptologists struggled to read hieroglyphs. The picture writing was very hard to understand and at first, some Egyptologists were not even sure that it was a form of writing at all. Then, in 1799, a young French soldier found a large slab of stone near the city of Rosetta in Egypt. It was almost a metre wide and more than a metre long, and it was covered in three types of writing – hieroglyphs, a type of later hieratic writing called demotic and an old type of Greek writing which they already knew how to read! Each of the languages said the same thing.

Egyptologists were able to use the stone, which they called the Rosetta Stone, to learn how to read hieroglyphs because they could compare it with the Greek and demotic writing. Once they had learned to read the Rosetta Stone, they were able to go on and discover what hieroglyphs written on other objects that had been discovered said.

FACT!
It took more than twenty years for Egyptologists to learn to read the Rosetta Stone, and many more years to read all the hieroglyphs that had been found before the stone's discovery.

ACTIVITY

Make a cartouche nameplate

A cartouche is a stretched circle, drawn to look like a rope, containing a person's name in hieroglyphs. When ancient Egyptians wrote a person's name inside a circle, it was believed that the circle protected the name, and the person. The names of pharaohs, gods and other important people were placed inside cartouches. You can make your own cartouche nameplate, to hang on your bedroom door!

You will need:
- 1 piece of thick white craft cardboard • scissors
- pencil and rubber • ruler
- silver and gold gel pens, or other colours of your choice
- piece of thin coloured craft cord about 150 cm long (available from craft stores) • glue

1. Use the ruler and pencil to measure out a square of cardboard around 40 cm long (depending on how long your name is) and 20 cm high. Then cut the square out.

2. Trim the four corners of the square so they are rounded in shape.

ACTIVITY

3. Use the ruler to draw a pencil line around 4 cm from the bottom of the cardboard. This will be your guide when writing your name.

4. Now use the pencil to carefully copy the hieroglyphs for each letter of your name onto the cardboard, from the chart below.

5. Colour the symbols in using the gel pens. When the ink is dry, rub out the pencil line you used as a guide.

6. Cut about 50 cm from the length of cord and put it aside. Then carefully glue the rest of the cord around the outer edges of your cartouche. Trim the ends of any leftover cord and leave to dry.

7. When the glue is dry, use the scissors to poke two holes in the top corners of the cartouche and thread the remaining 50 cm of cord through the holes, so you can hang the cartouche on your bedroom door!

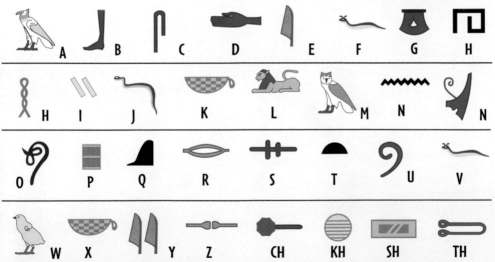

Papyrus Paper

The papyrus plant is a tall reed that grows along the banks of the River Nile. The ancient Egyptians used papyrus plants to make many different things. They made reed boats, sandals, baskets, mats and even ropes from papyrus. Papyrus was also burned in fires, as very few trees grew in ancient Egypt and wood was precious.

The most important use of papyrus in ancient Egypt was for making paper. The ancient Egyptians kept the method of making papyrus paper secret for a very long time, and sold the paper to other countries.

Papyrus paper was made by cutting material found inside the reeds into long strips, and pounding and soaking the strips. Then the strips were laid between two linen sheets in a criss-cross pattern. The strips were pressed between the two sheets and the water squeezed out, making a single sheet of paper.

FACT!
Many important ancient Egyptian documents were written on papyrus. They were found in the royal tombs by Egyptologists.

ACTIVITY

Make your own paper

Today, paper is made from wood pulp. You can recycle old paper and make your own new paper, using the method below. Then try writing some hieroglyphics on it!

You will need:

· Around 15 sheets of old office paper, ripped into small squares, or several handfuls of shredded white packing paper
· a blender · a large plastic tub · liquid starch or starch-based craft glue
· an old 20 cm x 25 cm picture frame with a sheet of nylon flyscreen tacked to it –
alternatively, you can stretch an old pair of nylon pantyhose over the frame
· warm water, a jug and a bucket · an iron · an adult's help

1. First, if you are using office paper, tear it up into small squares. Then place the office or packing paper in a bucket and fill it with water. Leave it to stand overnight.

2. The next day, carefully pour the water out of the bucket, leaving the softened paper behind.

ACTIVITY

3. Now you need to mash the paper up to turn it into pulp. Put one handful of paper into a kitchen blender, together with 500 ml warm water. Note: it's very important to ask an adult before using your family's kitchen blender and it's best to get an adult to help you with this part of the project.

4. Blend the water and paper together until it looks like thin porridge. If you have a small blender, use less paper and water.

5. Tip the blended paper pulp into the large tub. Repeat Step 4 until you have blended all your paper. Then rinse the blender out right away, so any remaining blended paper doesn't stick to it.

6. Add water to the paper pulp in the tub, until the tub is between $1/3$ and $1/2$ full. Then add two teaspoons of liquid starch, or starch-based glue. The starch will help seal the paper and make it easier to write on. This is called 'sizing' the paper.

ACTIVITY

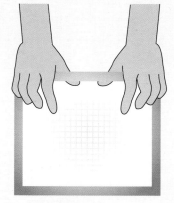

7. Then stir the pulp mixture until it is thoroughly mixed.

8. Now place the frame with flyscreen or pantyhose attached to it into the tub and swirl it around. Then gently lift it out of the water. You will see lots of paper fibres collect on top of the frame, forming a sheet of paper.

9. When you have an even coverage of paper on your frame, stand it in a warm sunny place while the paper dries. Then you can peel the paper off and start again. Alternatively, you can tip the frame upside-down onto a square of felt, and use the frame again immediately. However, this requires a lot of practice. You may like to try this when you are more experienced at paper making.

10. Once the paper has dried, ask an adult to help you press it firmly with an iron. Your paper is now ready to use!

TIP!
You can colour your paper with non-toxic powder paint. Add some yellow paint when you add the starch, to give the paper an ancient yellowed look.

The Gods of Ancient Egypt

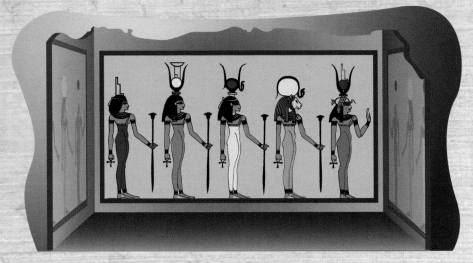

Ancient Egyptians were very religious people. They didn't just believe in one single god, but in many different gods and goddesses. There were gods and goddesses for different parts of the natural world, such as water, air, sky, land and animals. Gods and goddesses were also able to take human or animal form. They were often drawn as humans, with animal heads.

Some gods and goddesses were known and worshipped throughout the whole of ancient Egypt, while others were worshipped in only some towns or cities.

The kings of ancient Egypt were considered to be gods by their people. It was believed that after a king was crowned, he became a son of the most important god, Re.

Stories were told of gods and goddesses, and how they came into being. The stories were written on papyrus and inside tombs. Many tomb paintings show ancient Egyptian gods.

FACT!

The ancient Egyptian belief in gods and goddesses lasted for around three thousand years. Over time, new gods were created, or older gods became more or less important.

RE THE SUN GOD

*T*he most important god in ancient Egypt was Re, the sun god. Re was worshipped all over the country and was thought to be the father of all gods. Here is how the ancient Egyptians believed Re came into being, and created some of the other gods. There are several different versions of this story:

At the beginning of time, there was nothing but a huge, dark ocean. Then Re the sun god came out of a flower that was floating on the surface of the ocean. Re was alone in the world, so he created Shu, the god of the air, with his breath. Then he created Tefnut, the goddess of the air with his spittle. Shu and Tefnut had two children, Geb, the god of the earth and Nut, the goddess of the sky. The children of Nut and Geb became the stars in the sky.

The sun god Re had three different forms. He could be shown as a scarab beetle - a type of large beetle that is also known as the dung beetle - or, most often, as a round disc, or as an old man leaning on a stick.

FACT!
The sun god Re is sometimes called Ra.

HORUS
A VERY IMPORTANT GOD

*H*orus was one of ancient Egypt's oldest and most important gods. He was shown as a falcon, or a man with the head of a falcon. Horus was the son of two gods, Isis and Osiris. In ancient Egyptian stories Osiris was the king of Egypt. He was killed by his brother Seth, who was jealous of him for being such a good ruler. When Horus grew up he fought the evil Seth and claimed his father's throne. The other gods recognised Horus as the king of Egypt, rather than Seth. The eyes of Horus were said to be the sun and the moon. Ancient Egyptian kings were linked with Horus, as he was a brave warrior.

ISIS
WIFE AND MOTHER GODDESS

*I*sis was thought to be the brightest star in the sky, the dog star. This was called 'Soped' by the ancient Egyptians but we now know the star as Sirius. If you step outside at night in summer, you can clearly see Sirius. Ask an adult to help you find it! Isis was a very important goddess in Egypt and she was thought to be a very proud wife and mother. She protected her son, Horus, when he was attacked by Seth.

FACT!
Ancient Egyptians thought that when earthquakes happened, it was the earth god Geb laughing!

BASTET
A BEAUTIFUL CAT
GODDESS

Ancient Egyptians thought of cats as sacred animals. They trained them for hunting but they were also very useful for catching rats and mice, and keeping those pests out of the granaries (places where wheat and barley were stored). Cats were also made into mummies and placed in tombs, so they could travel to the afterlife and help the rulers who had died. The cat goddess Bastet was worshipped for her gentleness. However, if she was angered she could be shown as a lion, rather than a cat!

ANUBIS
THE JACKAL GOD

Anubis was a god with the head of a jackal (a type of wild dog). He was thought to be the god of the dead by ancient Egyptians. Anubis looked after dead people, watching over them as their bodies were embalmed and turned into mummies. He was their guide into the afterlife and protected their tombs. Beautiful statues of Anubis as a black dog have been found in the tombs of Egyptian kings, guarding the entrance to their tombs. One such statue was found in Tutankhamun's tomb. Ancient Egyptians valued dogs as pets and some mummified dogs have been found in their master's tombs, so the person could keep their pet in the afterlife.

FACT!
Ancient Egyptian dogs wore leather collars and were often shown in tomb paintings.

Tomb Paintings

*A*ncient Egyptians created many magnificent artworks - statues made of stone and wood, golden jewellery covered in precious stones, decorated jars and jugs, and beautiful paintings. Egyptians painted many large colourful murals inside the walls of royal tombs, called tomb paintings. Tomb paintings often showed scenes of daily life of the king or queen who was buried in the tomb, along with family members or Egyptian gods.

Tomb paintings always showed people looking their best – young and healthy. They never showed older people. This was because Egyptians believed that the paintings showed scenes from the person's afterlife, where everything had to be perfect. In fact, it was also believed that after the king or queen died, the tomb paintings might actually come to life, and show them in the way that they were now living!

FACT!

People shown in tomb paintings were not drawn to their actual size. The most important people were drawn as the largest people in the paintings, while people of less importance were drawn as smaller, even if in reality they were bigger.

ACTIVITY

Make an Egyptian-style mural

*A*ncient Egyptian tomb paintings were drawn using a grid system. First a picture was drawn on a small piece of wood, covered with a plaster grid. Then a large grid was drawn onto a tomb wall, and the picture copied onto it. You can make a cool Egyptian mural using the same method!

You will need:
• a pencil, ruler and rubber • a piece of paper around 15 cm x 15 cm
• a large piece of white craft paper or cardboard, around 100 cm x 100 cm
• coloured markers

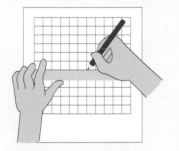

1. Draw a grid of 1 cm squares onto the piece of paper, with the pencil. Do 10 squares across and 10 squares down, as shown.

2. Now draw a grid of 10 cm squares onto the large piece of craft paper, with the pencil. Again, do 10 squares across and 10 squares down.

3. Draw an ancient Egyptian scene onto the small piece of paper. When you are happy with your drawing, copy it onto the large piece of paper, using the grid as a guide.

4. Colour your large drawing in with the markers, then rub out the remaining pencil lines. Your beautiful mural is finished!

Dress to Impress

Personal appearance was very important to ancient Egyptians, and they went to a lot of trouble to make sure that they looked good. Clothing was made from linen – a type of cloth made from fibres of the **flax** plant. Men wore a type of kilt that was wrapped around their waist. Sometimes they wore a loose type of shirt too. Women wore long dresses that came down to their ankles. Both men and women wore sandals made from papyrus reeds or leather.

Ancient Egyptians styled their hair in many different ways and fashions changed with the times, just as they do today. Sometimes they dyed their hair red with a dye called henna, which is still used today. At other times they wore head bands or decorative clips in their hair.

Young children had their heads shaved, except for a long piece of hair on one side of the head! Older boys sometimes shaved their heads, while girls liked to have long ponytails.

FACT!
Wigs were also very popular with ancient Egyptians. They were made of human hair or sheep's wool, and were very expensive.

*B*ecause the climate was very hot in Egypt, it was important to stay clean. Ancient Egyptians bathed and washed their hair regularly, and they went to a lot of trouble to smell nice. Scented flower petals and chips of cinnamon were often packed with wigs to keep them smelling good. Clothes were stored with scented flower petals, spices and a perfumed tree resin called frankincense.

One of the strangest things ancient Egyptians did to keep themselves smelling good was to place a special cone of scented fat on top of their heads, especially when going out to important events. The cones contained perfumed oils and ointments, which slowly melted into the ancient Egyptians' hair, or wigs. This kept them smelling good for hours!

Ancient Egyptians also rubbed perfumes, oils and ointments into their skin to keep themselves smelling good. They also did this to help keep their skin soft and stop it from drying out in the hot, dry Egyptian weather.

FACT!
Frankincense and myrrh, which is another type of resin from a plant, have been used since ancient times in perfumes and incense. They are still used today!

Ancient Egyptian Make-up

*B*oth men and women in ancient Egypt wore make-up, especially around their eyes. This can be seen in many tomb paintings. Men always shaved, using special brass razors, though some wore thin moustaches or beards. Too much hair on a man's face was considered unclean in those times!

Before going out, ancient Egyptians would first rub some scented oil or cream into their face to help keep it soft. Then they would apply lots of black eye make-up around the lids of their eyes, and also to their eyebrows. The black eye make-up, or kohl, was first made from soot. Later, it was made with a type of crushed lead ore.

Coloured eye make-up was also applied around the eyes, between the eyelids and the eyebrows. Blue and green were popular colours. They were both made from crushing a type of copper ore. Crushed eye shadow colours were ground together with plant gums or water to make a paste, and stored in little clay pots. They were applied with little round-ended sticks.

FACT!
Ladies in ancient Egyptian times also wore lipstick, which was probably made from a type of crushed red earth called ochre, mixed with fat.

ACTIVITY

Try ancient Egyptian make-up

*T*oday we have many make-up materials that are much safer and easier to use than those from ancient Egyptian times. You can use them to try some ancient Egyptian-style make-up. Check that it's okay to do this with an adult first. Mum or a big sister won't be happy if you use their make-up without permission!

You will need:

· mirror · face moisturising cream or sunscreen
· thick black eyeliner pencil · blue or green eye shadow
· red lipstick

1. First, wash and dry your face. Then rub a little face cream into your skin to soften it, just as the ancient Egyptians did. (These days sunscreen would be better if you want to protect your skin against hot, dry weather!)

2. Use the thick black eyeliner pencil to carefully draw around your eyes and to the sides of your head as shown, then use it to darken your eyebrows.

3. Colour the area between your eyelids in with the blue or green eye shadow.

4. If you are a girl, put on some red lipstick too. Now you have the ancient Egyptian look!

Beautiful Jewellery

Jewellery was very important to the people of ancient Egypt, and it was worn by both men and women. Rings, necklaces, bracelets, armbands and collars made from metals and gems were made by master craftsman. Many pieces of jewellery had small good luck charms, or amulets, threaded into them. They were believed to magically help keep the wearer safe from harmful spirits.

Poorer people in ancient Egypt wore jewellery made from pottery beads. Those who could afford it wore jewellery made from coloured glass beads, gemstones, silver, gold and other metals. Kings, queens and other royalty wore priceless jewellery made from solid gold, silver and rare gemstones.

When wealthy people died, beautiful pieces of jewellery were buried with them in their tombs. Many were stolen long ago by tomb raiders but some can be seen in museums today.

FACT!

Today, gold is worth much more than silver. At some times in ancient Egyptian history, silver was worth more than gold because it was harder to find at the time.

ACTIVITY

Make an ancient Egyptian necklace

Try making some of your own ancient Egyptian jewellery! Here's how.

You will need:

- around 60 cm nylon string (available from craft stores)
- a selection of medium-sized coloured beads (available from craft stores)
- six flower-shaped coloured beads (available from craft stores)

Lotus flowers were symbols of rebirth in ancient Egypt and often appeared in jewellery.

1. Tie a triple knot at the end of the nylon string, leaving 3 cm of string at the end to tie the necklace together when finished.

2. Carefully thread your selection of beads on to the string. The ancient Egyptians often used blue, red and black colours. You might like to do the same.

3. Thread a flower-shaped bead on around every 7 cm, so that the flowers are evenly spaced throughout the necklace.

4. When you have threaded the beads on the string, tie a knot 3 cm from the end of it. Check that the necklace will go over your head and then tie the two ends of the string together. Then your beautiful necklace will be finished!

Food, Ancient Egyptian Style

Ancient Egyptians were able to grow plenty of food along the banks of the River Nile. They grew grain crops such as wheat and barley, and harvested them each year. In fact they grew so much wheat that they often exported some of it to other neighbouring countries.

Bread was one of the most important foods for ancient Egyptians, and it was eaten daily. It was made from wheat flour and baked in special cone-shaped baking dishes over an open fire. Poorer people generally just ate plain bread, while wealthy people often added fruits or herbs to their breads to flavour it.

The ancient Egyptians did not know how to make sugar from sugar cane or sugar beets, so honey was collected and used to sweeten bread and other foods.

FACT!
Many ancient Egyptians had holes in their teeth, because grit and sand always got into their bread flour. Over time, the grit and sand in the bread wore the enamel on people's teeth away!

Ancient Egyptians ate several fruits and vegetables that we eat today. Delicious fruits such as dates and figs were eaten. Grapes, plums and watermelons were also on the menu. Fruits were often dried on the roofs of houses. Wealthy people could afford to eat more fruits than poorer people. Beans, some types of peas and onions were also part of the Egyptian diet.

The ancient Egyptians also ate several different types of meat. They hunted wild animals and birds in the marshes on the banks of the Nile. Wealthy people often went hunting, using throwing sticks that were a little like a boomerang to catch wild birds.

Beef was also eaten, from cattle raised by Egyptian farmers. There were lots of fish in the River Nile, and fish was caught and eaten by rich and poor people alike.

A type of beer was made from bread, honey and water for drinking. Wine was also made from grapes. Everyone drank beer but only wealthy people could afford to drink wine.

FACT!
Cats were trained for use in hunting in ancient Egypt, to help their owners catch wild birds.

ACTIVITY

Prepare an ancient Egyptian feast

*T*oday, we eat many of the delicious foods ancient Egyptians ate. You can prepare an ancient Egyptian feast for a group of your friends or your family! You will need an adult's permission and help for this activity.

You will need:
· 1 packet of dates · 1 packet of figs
· 1 bunch of grapes (or one packet of sultanas, which are dried grapes)
· several plums (or one packet of prunes, which are dried plums)
· 1/4 of a watermelon · 1 can of chick peas (these peas were eaten by ancient Egyptians)
· 1 lettuce · 1 loaf of plain bread · 1 fruit loaf
·honey · plates, dinner knives, serving bowls, tray and spoons

1. Ask an adult to take you to the supermarket to buy the ingredients for the feast. You may like to buy the bread from a bakery. Many ancient Egyptians made their own bread, but Egyptologists have discovered that some tomb workers were supplied with bread from a large bakery.

2. Wash the fresh fruits and cut the watermelon into pieces that can be held in the hand. Place the fresh fruits in serving bowls.

ACTIVITY

3. Wash and dry the lettuce, and place it in a serving bowl together with the chick peas (we do not know if ancient Egyptians ate their lettuce like this, but it tastes nice!).

4. Place the dried fruits in serving bowls.

5. Cut the breads into slices and place it on a serving tray, together with a bowl of honey. Guests can dip the bread in the honey. .

6. Ask your guests to sit at a table, as ancient Egyptians always stayed seated when eating at a feast. Give each guest a plate and then serve them, asking them what they would like to try. In ancient Egypt, serving girls served the food at feasts.

7. Allow your guests to eat with their fingers, as ancient Egyptians did. Knives and forks were not used in ancient Egypt.

8. Enjoy your feast!

FACT!
Egyptologists have learned much about ancient Egyptian feasts from descriptions written on papyrus and in tombs.

Fun and Games

A ncient Egyptians enjoyed playing lots of indoor and outdoor games, just as we do today. Egyptologists have learned a little about these games by studying papyrus texts and tomb paintings. Ancient board games have also been found inside tombs, as they were left there so that those who were buried in the tombs could continue to play the games in the afterlife.

A board game called Senet was very popular, especially among wealthy people. Senet was played on a board with three rows of ten squares, or holes. The rules of Senet were very complicated. Two people played and took turns by throwing sticks or knucklebones, instead of dice.

Dogs and Jackals was another popular board game. It was played on a board with many holes in it, and a palm tree in its centre. Pegs with the tops shaped like dogs and jackals seemed to have been raced across the board, although the exact rules of the game are not known.

Outdoor games using balls and sticks were also played. Balls and sticks were often made from papyrus reeds.

FACT!
Little is known about the rules of many Egyptian games. The rules have been lost in time!

ACTIVITY

Make your own board game

You can make a board game that looks similar to Dogs and Jackals.

You will need:

• coloured markers • small sheet of craft cardboard • scissors and glue
• two ice cream sticks • old shoebox with a lid • ruler • dice

1. First, make the 'dog' and 'jackal' game pieces. Draw a small dog's head and a small jackal's head the same size. Jackals are wild dogs with pointy ears and a pointy nose. Colour the dog and jackal in.

2. Use the glue to stick a dog's head on one ice cream stick and a jackal's head on the other.

3. Carefully poke fifteen holes on each side of the shoebox lid, then five more on each side curving back down, as shown. Use the ruler as a guide for the holes. Number the holes 1–20.

4. The game is ready! Two people can

play. The rules can be decided by you, but here is a suggestion. Each person takes a turn rolling the dice. They move their dogs or jackals along the holes, depending on the number they throw. However, if they throw a six, they go back to the beginning. The first to reach 20 wins!

FACT!

You may like to colour in the shoebox and perhaps draw a palm tree in the middle of it.

Learning More

Now that you have come to the end of this book, you can learn more about ancient Egypt by doing these things:

• Visit a museum near you. Most museums have works from ancient Egypt. Ring first, to be sure that they have some on display.

• Visit your local library and read some books on ancient Egypt.

• Ask an adult to help you find websites about ancient Egypt on the Internet. There are many good websites from museums around the world, with excellent pictures and information.

• When you are older, take a holiday to Egypt and visit some of the amazing pyramids, tombs and museums there!

GLOSSARY

ARCHAEOLOGISTS	people who study civilisations of the past
ARTEFACTS	objects or parts of objects made by people of the past
CONSTELLATIONS	patterns of stars in the sky, like the Southern Cross
DOCUMENTS	papers with writing on them, such as letters
EMBALMING	preserving a person or animal after they have died
EMPIRE	a group of countries ruled over by one ruler
FLAX	a plant with long thin leaves grown for its fibres
PHARAOHS	the name of the kings of ancient Egypt
TOMBS	burial places